Catechism of the Liturgy

The Mass of St. Giles
—The Master of St. Giles

A CATECHISM OF THE LITURGY

For Young and Old

Compiled from approved sources by

A Religious of the Sacred Heart

MEDIATRIX PRESS
MMXXIII

ISBN: 978-1-957066-40-0

©Mediatrix Press, 2023.

A Catechism of the Liturgy was originally published in 1919, and is in the public domain. Typesetting, additions and editing of this edition are the exclusive copyright of Mediatrix Press, all right's reserved. No part of this edition may reproduced or transmitted in any form or by any means, electronic or mechanical, including photocopying, recording, or by any information storage and retrieval system without permission in writing from the publisher. *No part of this work may be placed on Archive.org.*

Cover art, *Mass in St. John Lateran.* Villanueva

Nihil Obstat:
Die 7 Julii 1919.
Imprimatur;
25 Julii 1919.
ALOIS CAN, ATTARD, *Cens. Theol,*
+MAURAS, OS.B. *Arch. Epus. Melitae*

Nihil Obstat:
ARTHUR J. SCANLAN. S.T.D.
Cens. Librorum.
Imprimatur:
+ PATRICK J, HATES, D.D
Archbishop of New York
New York, July 19, 1921.

CONTENTS

THE LITURGY 15

THE LITURGICAL YEAR
Advent 63
Christmas 72
Lent 78
Holy Week 87
Easter to Advent 102

Foreword to the Mediatrix Press Edition

ONE of the tragic loses among the faithful during the last 60 years revolves around the knowledge of the richness of the Liturgical year and symbols contained in the liturgy of the Church.

As the ancient rite of Mass is recovered, the importance of the knowledge of the faithful of that richness needs to be recovered. This small catechism on the liturgy provides a good foundation in the various elements of the liturgy and the meanings behind them. Even many traditional priests are unaware of many things contained in this small text, and so this book serves to provide that knowledge so that a full appreciation of the tradition of the Church regarding its liturgy may be recovered.

One joy that a Catholic often

receives in relation to well written catechisms is the clarity which is contained therein. This catechism gives clear and concise explanations of various elements of the liturgy, rounding out one's lack of knowledge and giving clarity to the meanings of each element discussed. The reader would be well suited to study the explanation given herein, since it puts him in contact with the longstanding tradition of the Catholic Church and its liturgy.

Fr. Chad Ripperger, PhD

FOREWORD
to the 1919 Edition

THIS little work deserves a warm welcome from Catholic Schools and homes, for it gives in small compass the rudiments of a subject which has been too little studied amongst us, but which is happily regaining its lawful place. This growing appreciation is a matter for congratulation, for where the Liturgy of the Church is loved and lived, Christian principles are sure to be vigorous.

The Liturgy is the form of public worship prescribed and arranged by the Church, Theology teaches that the Church is a living body, an organism, which has the duty of offering, as a body, praise and sacrifice to Almighty God, and for the fulfillment of this duty the Church has designed a form of prayers and actions, which we call the Liturgy. The Liturgy, then, is the official prayer of the Church. In it she offers to God homage and expiation, draws down His blessings, renders Him thanks. Through it she sanctifies every part of the day and night, and converts the whole year into a continuous circle of prayer. This center is formed by the Holy Mass, in which the Adorable Sacrifice is surrounded by a magnificent set of prayers and actions. Round the Mass, in a wider circle, we have the Canonical Hours, *i,* e., forms of prayer distributed over the hours of day and night. Then dividing the mystery of the divine work of the Redemption into its various phases, as the prism divides the light into colors, it establishes a series of festivities encircling the whole year.

Through Advent, with its sombre but joyful expectation, we are led to Christmas, which is followed by the

A Catechism of the Liturgy

austere periods of Septuagesima and Lent, preparation for the holiest seasons of Passion tide and Easter. Paschaltide gives us a long extension of the joy of the Resurrection, and ends with the crowning festival of Pentecost. Then, with new sets of offices, we are led on, week by week, to another Advent. With such inspiration the Christian life is nurtured, mentally and morally, and the true Catholic character is formed.

We can frame no better wish for this little catechism than that it may serve as an introduction to the Church's treasure-house.

Stanbrook Abbey, Worcester.
November 20, 1919

A CATECHISM OF THE LITURGY

THE LITURGY

1. What is the meaning of the word Liturgy?

Originally it meant a public duty, a service to the State, undertaken freely by a citizen. The meaning is extended to cover general service of a public kind.

2. Where is the word first used in Scripture?

In the Septuagint it is used for the public service of the temple (Exodus 38). Thence it comes to have a religious sense as the function of the priests, the ritual service of the Temple (Joel).

3. What does the term Liturgy now include?

The whole complex order of

official services, all the Rites, Ceremonies, prayers and Sacraments of the Church as opposed to private devotions.

4. How could you find out which services are Liturgical?

Those services are Liturgical which are contained in any of the official books of a Rite: e, g., Compline is a Liturgical service, the Rosary is not.

5. In what sense is the word Liturgy used in the Greek Church?

The Greek Church restricts it to the chief official service—the Sacrifice of the Holy Eucharist which in our Rite we call the Mass. When a Greek speaks of the Holy Liturgy he means only the Eucharistic service.

6. What do you mean by

Liturgical Books?

The Liturgical Books are all the Books published by the authority of the Church, that contain the text and directions for her official services.

7. Name the Liturgical Books.

The Liturgical Books are: The Missal, the Pontifical, the Breviary, the Ritual, the Bishop's Ceremonial, the Memorial of Rites, and the Martyrology.

8. When was the Roman Missal first published?

The Roman Missal as we now have it, was published by St. Pius V in 1570. It has been revised in several succeeding Pontificates, new Masses have been added according to need, but it is still that of Pius V.

9. What does the text of the Missal contain?

The first part contains the "Proper of the Season" from the first Sunday of Advent to the last after Pentecost. The proper of each Mass is given in order of the ecclesiastical year, that is the Masses of each Sunday and other days (vigils, ember days, etc.) that have a proper Mass. Certain rites not Eucharistic, but connected closely with the Mass are in their place in the Missal, such as the blessing of ashes, candles, palms; all the morning services of Holy Week (except the Vespers of Thursday and Friday). After the service of Holy Saturday the whole Ordinary of the Mass with the Canon is inserted.

10. What is the Ordinary of the Mass?

The Ordinary is that part of the Mass which does not change except for the thirteen proper Prefaces and the few changes that occur in the

Canon. After the Ordinary comes Easter Day and the rest of the year in order.

11. What does the second part of the Missal contain?

It contains the Proper of Saints, that is, the feasts that occur through the year. It begins with the Vigil of St. Andrew, which generally falls at the beginning of Advent.

12. What does the third part contain?

It contains the Common Masses, that is, general Masses for Apostles, Martyrs, ,etc. Masses for the dead, Supplements, i.e. a collection of Votive Masses, special Masses for certain dioceses.

13. What is the Pontifical?

The Pontifical is the Bishop's book, and contains the rites of

Confirmation, Ordination, Blessing of Abbots, consecration of Churches, Altars, Chalices, etc.

14. What is the Breviary?

The Breviary contains all the Divine Office without Chant. It is divided into four parts:[1] Winter, Spring, Summer, Autumn. It contains the Psalter, hymns, readings, as well as antiphons and prayers said according to the season and the liturgical year.

15. What is the Psalter?

The Psalter is the most ancient and venerable part of the breviary, containing all 150 Psalms distributed to the canonical hours and recited in the space of one week.

---

[1] It was later combined into two volumes in 1962.

16. What is the Divine Office?

The Divine Office, at present, refers to the Church's official liturgical prayer at the canonical hours, whether recited publicly in choir or privately.

17. What is Choir?

In the liturgy, the word Choir refers to the stalls in the Church where clergy and religious recite the divine office.

18. Why is the phrase "Divine Office" used?

The phrase "Divine Office" signifies the duty (*officium*) accomplished for God by the Church. Strictly speaking it is used to refer to the recitation of psalms and prayers at certain hours (called canonical hours) as they are found today in the breviary.

19. By whom is the Divine Office said?

The Divine Office is said by all Priests and by the members of religious orders, both of men and women.

20. May the laity, and those who have no obligation to do so pray the divine office?

The laity not only may, but are encouraged as much as their state in life permits to join the Church in praying the Divine Office.

21. What are the Canonical hours?

As each day has its own office, it is also divided into Hours founded on the ancient Roman divisions of the day. The hours are Matins and Lauds, Prime, Terce, Sext, None, Vespers and Compline.

22. What is Matins?

Matins is called the night office, but is said in early morning (*Matutinae*). It is divided into three nocturns, corresponding to the three watches after midnight. At present, each nocturn consists of three Psalms, and on feast days three readings; it concludes with the *Te Deum*.

23. What is the office of Lauds?

Lauds is said either immediately after Matins, or a period following it, normally at dawn. It is comprised of five psalms, a chapter, hymn, and the Benedictus.

24. What is the Benedictus?

The Benedictus is the canticle sung by St. Zachary after the birth of his son, St. John the Baptist (Lk. 1:68-79). It is sung or said before the concluding prayer at every office of

Lauds.

25. What are the "little hours" (*horae minores*)?

The little hours are Prime, Terce, Sext, and None. Their names come from the Latin reckoning of time, which correspond roughly to 7am, 9am, 12pm, and 3pm, although their actual time of celebration may differ or be anticipated. Each hour contains a hymn, three psalms, and a short chapter.

26. What is Vespers?

Vespers is the evening office, comprised of five psalms, a chapter, hymn, and the Magnificat. On feast days, there is a first and second vespers, the first beginning on the eve of the feast, and the second to conclude it.

27. What is the Magnificat?

The Magnificat is the canticle which the Blessed Virgin Mary sings in Lk. 1:46-55, and it is said or sung in every celebration of Vespers of the year.

28. What is Compline?

Compline is the last office of the night, added formally by St. Benedict in his *Rule*. It comprises a confession of sins, three psalms, a chapter, the canticle Nunc Dimittis (Lk. 2:29-32), and one of the Marian Antiphons.

29. What are the Marian Antiphons?

The Marian Antiphons are special hymns to the Blessed Virgin Mary which are sung at compline. They comprise of the *Alma Redemptoris Mater* (Advent/Christmas), *Ave Regina Caelorum* (Lent), *Regina Coeli* (Easter), and *Salve Regina* (Time after Pentecost).

30. What does the Ritual contain?

The Ritual contains all the services a priest needs beside those of the Missal and Breviary; directions for the administration of the various Sacraments, processions, funerals, exorcisms, etc.

31. What does the Ceremonial of Bishops contain?

In spite of its title it contains much matter needed by other people than Bishops. It contains general directions for Episcopal functions, and for the Bishop's attendants, full directions for everything connected with Mass, Divine Office, its chanting in Choir and the ritual belonging to it. It is an indispensable supplement to the rubrics of the Missal, Breviary, Ritual and Pontifical.

32. What is the Memorial of Rites?

The Memorial of Rites or the Little Ritual gives direction for certain rites, blessing of candles, ashes, palms, etc., in. small churches where there is neither deacon nor subdeacon.

33. What is the Martyrology?

It is an enlarged calendar giving the names, and very short accounts of all saints (not martyrs only) commemorated in various places each day. If it is sung in choir, it is during the office of Prime. Otherwise it is read during meals in monasteries and other religious institutes.

34. Name the Liturgical colors?

White, Red, Green, Violet and Black are Liturgical colors.

35. What is meant by Chant?

In the strict sense "Chant" means

a melody executed by the human voice only; in a wider sense the word is taken to mean such singing even when accompanied by instruments; it may also mean instrumental music alone.

36. What is Liturgical Chant?

Liturgical Chant means Liturgical or Sacred music. Sacred music embodies four distinct, but subordinate, elements: plain chant; harmonized chant; one or other of these accompanied by organ and instruments; and organ and instruments alone.

37. What is meant by plain chant?

This name only came into use in the twelfth and thirteenth centuries, it was given to the old church music to distinguish it from the "musica mensurata" which began to be developed at that time. Plain chant is synonymous with Gregorian or Roman Chant, by which is now meant not only early Church Music, but all similar compositions written to the end of the sixteenth century and even later.

38. Why is the Roman Chant also called Gregorian?

The Roman Chant is also called Gregorian because this dignified and solemn Chant was taught and brought to perfection in a school founded by St. Gregory the Great for which he gave land and two houses. He collected into one volume, called the *Antiphonary* all that was to be sung during Mass and other church ceremonies. He wished these chants to be spread through the whole Latin Church. He is said to have himself presided at the lessons given and even to have taught the younger children himself. When they were

A Catechism of the Liturgy

sufficiently instructed he sent his scholars to both England and France. Two centuries later the Chants sent by Pope Adrian to Charlemagne came from this Gregorian School of Music.

39. What is meant by extra-Liturgical music?

The music which accompanies non-Liturgical functions of Catholic worship is usually and accurately styled extra-Liturgical. Music for these functions should assume as far as possible the character without the extreme severity of Liturgical music.

40. Which are the principal Liturgies in use in the Eastern Church in the present day?

The Liturgy of St. John Chrysostom in its Slavonic form, is used by the Russian church in Russia itself. It is also used in Greece and by the Bulgarians, Albanians, Ruthenians, etc., as well as by the United Greeks of the four patriarchates and some others.

41. Is this the only Liturgy used in these places?

No, the Liturgy of St. Basil is used on certain days in the year instead of that of St. Chrysostom.

42. Which are the Liturgies of the Western church?

With the exception of a few rites, the Roman Liturgy has universal sway.

43. Which other rites are used in the West?

The Ambrosian Liturgy is used in Milan and the Mozarabic Liturgy in Toledo in Spain.

44. What do you know of these

Liturgies?

The Ambrosian Liturgy, so-called from St. Ambrose, Bishop of Milan A. D. 374, is very ancient. The Milanese say it is the work of St. Barnabas, Apostle. Many attempts have been made to abolish this rite and to substitute the Roman, but to no purpose.

45. What are some of the particularities of this rite?

It allows no "Agnus Dei" except in Masses for the Dead, On Easter Sunday two Masses are prescribed, one for the newly baptized and one for the feast and throughout the whole of Lent there is no Mass on Friday.

46. What is the Mozarabic rite?

The Mozarabic rite is a survival of the Gothic Liturgy that was formerly in use throughout Spain but is now restricted to the city of Toledo only.

47. What was the Sarum rite?
The Sarum rite prevailed throughout Great Britain generally, until the reign of Edward VI when the Catholic Mass was suppressed and replaced by the Protestant book of Common Prayer. After the restoration of Catholicism under Queen Mary in 1553, it enjoyed a short life before it was again suppressed by Elizabeth I through the reimposition of the book of Common Prayer.

48. How did the Sarum rite originate?
The Sarum rite was introduced by St. Osmund, Bishop of Sarum, in Wiltshire, England, in 1078, and was renowned for the magnificence of its ceremonies.

49. Which of the Religious Orders have rites of their own?

Four Religious Orders have rites of their own, namely the Carthusians, Premonstratensians (Norbertines), Carmelites, and the Dominicans.

50. What are some of the different kinds of Mass?

Solemn High Mass, is celebrated with deacon and subdeacon and a number of inferior ministers. It is called "High" from the fact that the greater part is chanted in a high tone of voice.

51. What is a Missa Cantata?

A Missa Cantata or simple sung Mass is so called when there is neither deacon nor subdeacon.

52. What is a Low Mass?

A Low Mass is so called from its being said without deacon and subdeacon and without the usual marks of solemnity of a High Mass.

53. What is a conventual Mass?

A conventual Mass, strictly speaking, is that which the canons attached to a Cathedral are required to celebrate daily after the hour of Terce—that is—about 9 o'clock.

54. What is a Nuptial Mass?

A Nuptial or Bridal Mass is a special service set apart in the Missal for the Bridegroom and Bride and which has a few ceremonies peculiar to it alone. It is of very ancient origin and has the singular rite of interrupting the Canon itself after the Pater Noster to pronounce a blessing over the newly married pair.

55. What is meant by a Golden Mass?

The Golden Mass was one that used to be celebrated formerly on the

Wednesday of the Quarter Tense of Advent in honor of the Mother of God. It was a solemn High Mass of the most gorgeous kind and often lasted three or four hours. The Bishop and all his canons assisted at it. At the Church of St. Guduld, in Brussels, this Mass is celebrated every year on the twenty-third of December.

56. What is a votive Mass?

A votive Mass is a Mass not in accordance with the office of the day. As every day in the year has a Mass peculiar to itself, whenever this order is broken in upon, the Mass said instead is called votive, or a Mass of devotion. Votive Masses may not be celebrated on Sundays or within the octaves of Christmas, Epiphany, Easter, Pentecost, Corpus Christi nor in Holy Week. The "Gloria in Excelsis" and the Creed are omitted in votive Masses, and a commemoration is always made of the Mass of the day.

57. What exception is there in regard to the "Gloria" in votive Masses?

In the votive Mass of the Angels and in the Saturday votive Mass of Our Blessed Lady, the "Gloria in Excelsis" is allowed.

58. When is Midnight Mass allowed?

Midnight Mass is now only allowed at Christmas, but midnight Masses used to be common during times of persecution, and later on certain festivals had the privilege of Midnight Mass.

59. What is a Requiem Mass?

A Requiem Mass is a Mass for the dead.

60. When may a Requiem Mass be celebrated?

Requiem Masses are accustomed to be said: 1st. When a person dies, or on any day between the day of the death and that of the burial; 2nd. on the third day after death, in memory of Our Lord's Resurrection; 3d. on the seventh day; 4th. on the thirtieth day; 5th. at the end of a year, that is on the anniversary day.

61. What is the altar?

The altar is the sacred table on which Mass is offered. Before Mass may be celebrated on it, it must first be consecrated by the Bishop.

62. What is meant by the right and left sides of the altar?

The right and left sides of the altar are so called from the right and left hands of the crucifix so that the right side is the Gospel side and the left side is the Epistle side. Up to the fifteenth century it used to be just the opposite according to the right and left hand of the priest.

63. How must the altar be covered?

It is of strict obligation that every altar upon which the Holy Sacrifice is offered should be covered with three linen cloths. Before these cloths are used they must be blessed by the Bishop or by one of his delegates.

64. Why are three altar cloths used?

Three altar cloths are used in honor of the Blessed Trinity, as well as to commemorate the linen cloths in which Our Lord's Body was wrapped in the sepulchre.

65. Why are relics of Saints

placed in the altar?

Relics of Saints are placed in the altar because in the time of persecution it was customary to say Mass on the tombs of the Martyrs. When peace was restored to the Church this custom gradually gave way to that of laying in the newly consecrated altars some portion of the Martyrs' bodies.

66. Who places the relics of the Martyrs in the altar?

The Bishop, who consecrates the altar, places the relics in it.

67. What must be on the altar whenever Mass is said?

There must be, besides the three altar cloths, a crucifix and two lighted candles and usually a Missal. Missal-stand and three altar cards.

68. What is the meaning of the

Word "Doxology"?

The minor Doxology means a word of praise or glory. Doxology is the "Glory be to the Father," and the major Doxology is the "Gloria in Excelsis."

69. How many languages are used in the Mass?

Three languages are used in the Mass: Latin, Greek and Hebrew.

70. Why are these three languages used?

Because the title of the Cross was written in these three languages.

71. Which are the Greek and Hebrew words used in the Mass?

The Greek words are "Kyrie Eleison" and "Agios o Theos, etc.," on Good Friday; and the Hebrew words are *Hosannah, Sabaoth, Alleluia, Amen, Seraphim* and *Cherubim*.

72. How many Collects are allowed in the Mass?

It is forbidden to say more than seven Collects at any time, and this number is rarely said. On great feasts, only one is said but on ordinary occasions three is the usual number.

73. Why is the Gradual so called?

The Gradual is so called not as some suppose from the steps of the altar, for it was never read there, but rather from the steps of the ambo.

74. What was the ambo?

The ambo was an elevated lectern or pulpit placed generally in the nave of the church from which the epistle used to be read or chanted. Specimens of these may yet be seen in the ancient Church of San Clemente in Rome.

75. What is a Sequence?

A Sequence is a rhythmical composition which on certain occasions in the year is added immediately after the Gradual.

76. What other names are given to Sequences?

Sequences are also called proses (*prosa*) or jubilations.

77. What is the reason of these names?

They are called "proses" because, though in verse, they have not the qualities of regular metrical compositions, *i,* e., more attention is paid to accent than to quantity. The name "jubilation" was given for their being employed for the most part on occasions of great solemnity and rejoicing; and because the musical phrase following the Allel, to which the early Sequences were set, was called a *jubilus* the name Sequence came from their following the "alleluia."

78. How many Sequences have now a place in the Mass?

There are only five Sequences; 1st. The "Victimae Paschali," proper to Easter; 2d. the "Veni Sancte Spiritus," proper to Pentecost; 3d. the "Lauda Sion," proper to Corpus Christi; 4th. The "Stabat Mater," proper to the feast of the Seven Dolors of the Blessed Virgin Mary; 5th. the "Dies Irae," proper to Masses for the dead.

79. What do you know of the authorship of any of these Sequences?

The "Veni Sancte Spiritus" is generally ascribed to Blessed Hermann Contractus or the Cripple; by others it is ascribed to Pope Innocent III. and to Robert, King of the Franks.

80. Who composed the "Lauda Sion"?

The "Lauda Sion" was composed by St. Thomas Aquinas at the request of Pope Urban IV.

81. Who was the author of the "Stabat Mater"?

The "Stabat Mater" is generally ascribed to Jacopone da Todi, a Franciscan Friar.

82. What was the Discipline of the Secret?

The "Disciplina Arcana," or Discipline of the Secret, was the custom which prevailed in the Church during the first five centuries, of carefully concealing the principal mysteries of Our Holy Faith from pagans and Catechumens, and those were therefore dismissed before the most solemn part of the Mass began.

83. What is meant by the Mass of the Faithful?

The Catechumens were dismissed from Mass the moment the sermon was finished at the end of the Gospel, and then the Mass of the Faithful began with closed doors.

84. Who also were dismissed besides Catechumens?

Besides the Catechumens there were also dismissed those troubled with unclean spirits; the lapsed, or those who openly denied the faith; public sinners whose term of penance had not yet expired, and Jews, Gentiles and pagans.

85. What is meant by the Mass of the Catechumens?

The Mass of the Catechumens means that part of the Mass when

Catechumens might be present, that is, up to the sermon.

86. On what feasts is the Creed said at Mass?

The Creed is said on all Sundays of the year, feasts of Our Lord, the Blessed Virgin, the Holy Angels, the Apostles, and Doctors of the Church. The only woman saint besides the Blessed Virgin who has a Creed in her Mass is St. Mary Magdalene because she was the "Apostle of the Apostles."

87. What old dictum gives the feasts upon which the Creed is not said at Mass?

The dictum, "MUC NON CREDUNT," M stands for Martyrs, U or V for Virgins, widows and non-virgins, C for Confessors, all of whom have no Creed special to them.

88. What is the origin of the Nicene Creed?

The Nicene Creed was framed in the year 325 at the general Council of Nicea, a town of Bithynia in Asia Minor, where three hundred and eighteen Fathers assembled at the call of Pope Sylvester, to condemn the heretic Arius, who denied the Divinity of Our Lord.

89. Which was the principal clause inserted in the Creed by the Fathers?

"Consubstantial with the Father" was the clause which took away from Arius the last prop on which his heresy rested.

90. When was the Creed further added to?

The Nicene Creed was added to at the Council of Constantinople A. D. 381, which condemned the heresy of

Macedonius, who denied the Divinity of the Holy Ghost.

91. How many Prefaces are in use in the Roman Church now?

The number of Prefaces in use in the Roman Church is thirteen: 1st. The Preface of the Nativity; 2d. of the Epiphany; 3d. of Lent; 4th. of the Cross and Passion; 5th. of Easter Sunday; 6th. of the Ascension; 7th. of Pentecost; 8th. of the Blessed Trinity, used on every Sunday; 9th. of the Blessed Virgin; 10th. of the Apostles; 11th. of St. Joseph; 12th. of the Dead, 13th. Of the Common.

92. What is the meaning of the word Canon?

The word CANON in Greek signified a straight rod, then a rule used by masons and carpenters for measuring; now, by a metaphor, it is used as a rule in art, and accordingly the sense of something fixed is found in the various uses of the word Canon as applied by the Church.

93. What are some of the uses of the word Canon?

The Canon of Scripture is the fixed list of books which the Church recognizes as inspired. Ecclesiastical laws and definitions of councils are called CANONS and are the fixed rules of faith or conduct. CANONIZATION is the inscribing the name of a Servant of God on a fixed list of Saints whom the Church places on her altars. CANON as an ecclesiastical dignity, means originally one on a fixed list of clerics attached to a church or a cathedral.

94. What is the Canon of the Mass?

The Canon of the Mass means the fixed rules according to which the

Holy Sacrifice is offered. It means the fixed portion of the Mass. Its present form was arranged chiefly by St. Gregory the Great.

95. What is meant by the term, "Within the Action"?

The Canon was sometimes called by ancient writers the Action or the Great Act of the priest, as it included the consecration of the Bread and Wine, changing them into the Body and Blood of Our Lord. The words, "Within the Action," are now applied to the prayer in the Canon which begins with the word, "Communicantes."

96. What is to be noticed about the prayer, "Communicantes"?

Although this prayer is part of the Canon of the Mass which is otherwise never changed, an addition is made to it on five great feasts of the year: Christmas, Epiphany, Easter, Ascension, and Pentecost.

97. What Saints are mentioned by name in the Canon of the Mass before the Consecration?

Before the Consecration there are mentioned by name, the Blessed Virgin, the twelve Apostles and twelve Martyrs, the first five of whom were Popes.

98. Which of the Apostles is omitted from the list?

St. Matthias is omitted because he was not an Apostle at the time of Our Lord's Passion and St. Paul is inserted, though not one of the twelve Apostles as he is always united to St. Peter in the Liturgy of the Church.

99. Name the five Popes mentioned in the Canon?

A Catechism of the Liturgy

SS. Linus, Cletus, Clement, Xystus and Cornelius, the first three of whom were fellow laborers with St. Peter.

100. Which are the other Martyrs, not Popes, mentioned at this place in the Canons?

St. Cyprian, Bishop of Carthage; SS. Lawrence, Chrysogonus, John and Paul, brothers; Cosmos and Damian, also brothers and physicians.

101. What persons of the Old Testament are mentioned in the Ordinary of the Mass?

Abel, Abraham, Melchisedech and Isaias are mentioned in the Ordinary of the Mass.

102. Are any women Saints mentioned in the Canon?

Yes, SS. Felicitas, Perpetua, Agatha, Lucy, Agnes, Cecilia and

Anastasia are mentioned in the Canon after the Consecration.

103. What custom formerly prevailed at the Memento of the living and of the dead?

Up to the twelfth century in the Latin Church it was customary to read aloud from the diptychs the names of those to be prayed for.

104. What were the diptychs?

Diptychs were tablets on which were inscribed the names of the living and the dead, and the deacon read them aloud from the ambo. In the Mozarabic rite the custom of the reading of the diptychs is still in use.

105. What was the origin of the elevation of the Host after the Consecration?

The present custom of the elevation of the Host after the

Consecration dates from the eleventh century and was introduced as a protest against the heretic Berengarius, who denied the doctrine of transubstantiation.

106. What is the minor or little elevation?

The minor elevation takes place a little before the "Pater Noster" at the words, "omnis honor et gloria," when the priest raises the chalice and Host a few inches from the altar. This used to be the only elevation.

107. How many ceremonies is the priest obliged to observe while saying Mass?

The priest has to observe 500 ceremonies while saying Mass, besides 400 rubrics, which makes in all 900 obligations which he is bound to observe under pain of sin.

A Catechism of the Liturgy

108. What are some of the ceremonies he is hound to observe?

He has to turn six times towards the people, to kiss the altar eight times, to raise his eyes to heaven eleven times, and to strike his breast ten times in Masses for the Living, seven times in Masses for the Dead.

109. How many times does the priest join his hands and bow his head during Mass?

He joins his bands fifty-four times and bows his head twenty-one times; and he puts both hands on the altar twenty-nine times.

110. How many times does the priest make the sign of the cross?

The priest makes the sign of the cross thirty-three times over the offering, sixteen times on himself and twice when he turns and blesses the people; once on the book; and he makes the sign of the cross with the Host before he gives Holy Communion to each communicant.

111. What are some of the differences between a High Mass and a Low Mass?

High Mass differs from Low Mass merely by way of addition. Music is of obligation, the Gospel is solemnly chanted by the deacon and the Epistle by the subdeacon. The altar and the people are incensed, and the Pax or Kiss of Peace is given by the priest to the deacon and by him to the subdeacon after the Pater Noster.

112. Which parts of a High Mass are sung by the choir?

The choir sings the Introit, Kyrie, Gloria, Gradual, Creed, Offertory, Sanctus, and Benedictus, Agnus Dei and Communion.

113. What powers does a deacon receive at Ordination?

The deacon at Ordination receives the power of assisting the priest at High Mass, of solemnly singing the Gospel, of preaching, and of administering solemn baptism.

114. How does the deacon wear the stole?

The deacon wears the stole across the left shoulder instead of crossed in front like the priest.

115. How does a Mass for the Dead differ from a Mass for the Living?

Chiefly by way of omission—The psalm "Judica me," is omitted—also the Gloria and Creed as in other votive Masses. At the Agnus Dei the words, "Dona eis requiem," are substituted for "Miserere nobis" and before the last Gospel instead of saying, "Ite Missa est," the words, "Requiescat in pace," are said, and the priest's blessing is not given.

116. What is the special advantage of a Requiem Mass?

So far as the essence of the Sacrifice is concerned, all Masses are equal, but the prayers in the Requiem Mass are said in the Church's name and by the Church's order, and consequently obtain special graces for the departed.

117. Mention some differences between a Bishop's Mass and a priest's Mass.

The Bishop vests at the altar. He receives the maniple only at the "Indulgentiam" after the Confiteor. He says "Pax Vobis" after the Gloria instead of the "Dominus Vobiscum." At the blessing the Bishop makes three signs of the cross over the people. In the first prayer of the Canon, instead of saying the words, "our Bishop N.," he says, "and I Thy unworthy servant." He is always assisted by a priest.

118. What is a Pontifical Mass?

A Pontifical Mass is the solemn High Mass celebrated by a Bishop. The full ceremonial is carried out when he celebrates at the throne in his own Cathedral Church or with permission at the throne in another diocese.

119. What are some of the ceremonials?

The Canons assist in their vestments, besides priests, deacons and subdeacons. Nine acolytes or clerics minister the book, bugia, mitre, crosier, censer, two candles, gremiale and cruets and four minister in turn at the washing of the Bishop's hands. There should also be a train-bearer and at least four torch-bearers at the Elevation.

120. What are the ornaments worn by a Bishop or Archbishop besides the usual Mass vestments?

The ornaments worn by a Bishop or an Archbishop are the buskins, sandals, pectoral cross, tunic, dalmatic, gloves, pallium, mitre, ring, crosier which he carries and the gremiale or apron.

121. What peculiar ceremonies has the solemn Pontifical Mass celebrated by the Pope in St. Peter's?

In a Papal Mass a Cardinal Bishop acts as assistant priest — Cardinal Deacon is the deacon of the Mass, and an auditor of the Rota is subdeacon. The Epistle and Gospel are sung first in Latin and then in Greek. While elevating the Host and the Chalice the Pope turns in a half circle towards the Epistle and Gospel side. The Pope receives Communion standing at the throne, the deacon bringing him the Chalice and the subdeacon the paten with the Host.

122. What privilege is retained in the Pope's solemn Mass at the tombs of the Apostles?

The deacon and subdeacon are privileged to partake of the Precious Blood from the Chalice. This is the only survival of a usage which was almost universal in the Church for eleven hundred years.

THE LITURGICAL YEAR

ADVENT

123. Why are the weeks preparatory to Christmas called Advent?

From the Latin word, "Adventus," which means coming.

124. When did the custom of keeping Advent originate?

The custom of keeping Advent originated in the fourth century in the churches of the East. It was only towards the end of that century that the date of Christmas was fixed for December 25th.

125. When is the first Sunday

A Catechism of the Liturgy

of Advent?

The first Sunday of Advent is the Sunday nearest to the Feast of St. Andrew, November 30th.

126. How is Advent kept?

Advent is kept by special prayer.

127. What is the earliest proof of special Advent exercises?

In a passage of St. Gregory of Tours' *History of the Franks* we find that St. Perpetuus, one of his predecessors in the See, had decreed in A. D. 480 that the faithful should fast three times a week from the feast of St. Martin (November 11th) to Christmas.

128. What was this period called?

This period was called St. Martin's Lent and his feast was kept with the same kind of rejoicing as Carnival.

129. When did this original observance of Advent cease?

Probably in the twelfth century, but the change was gradual and in time Advent came to be observed in its now modified form.

130. Which are the three "comings" of Our Lord so often alluded to in the Liturgy for Advent?

1st. His coming in the Incarnation. 2d. His coming to each soul. 3d, His coming at the Last Judgment.

131. What does St. Bernard say of these comings?

He says, in the first Our Lord comes in the weakness of human nature; in the second, He comes in spirit and with power; in the third He comes in glory and in majesty.

132. What connection is there

between the first coming and the length of Advent?

The world waited four thousand years for the Incarnation, while we wait four weeks spent in special preparation.

133. What color is worn for church functions during Advent?

Purple is worn except on feast-days. This color shows with what sincerity the Church unites herself in spirit with the true Israelites who waited, in sackcloth and ashes, the coming of the Messiah.

134. What omission is there in the Ordinary of the Mass during Advent?

Except on the feast-days of Saints, the "Gloria in Excelsis" is omitted and instead of "Ite Missa est" the priest says "Benedicamus Domino."

135. Is Advent a time of mourning then?

No, because though the "Gloria in Excelsis" and the "Te Deum" are not said, the "Alleluias" are continued.

136. Where is the station for the first Sunday in Advent?

In the Church of St. Mary Major under the protection of Our Lady and in this basilica where the Manger is kept, the Church begins Advent.

137. What is meant by the word station as used in the Missal?

The stations marked in the Missal, refer to former times when the clergy and people of Rome went in procession to the particular church named for that day and there said office and celebrated or assisted at Mass.

138. Where is the station of the second Sunday?

In the Church of the Holy Cross in Jerusalem, one of the oldest churches in Rome. Here the relics of the True Cross with the title, "Presented by Constantine the Great to this Church" are kept with great care.

139. Is there anything special about the third Sunday?

The third Sunday is called "Gaudete" because of the first word in the Introit; the organ is played, the priest wears a rose-colored vestment and the deacon and subdeacon wear dalmatic and tunic respectively. In the Cathedral the Bishop assists wearing the mitre, known as "precious" (*i.e.*, a mitre adorned with precious stones). The station is at St. Peter's.

140. When do the Advent

Ember Days occur?

The Advent Ember Days occur on the Wednesday, Friday and Saturday after the third Sunday in Advent.

141. When did this custom originate?

From the very first centuries, the Church set apart three days in each of the four seasons as special days of petition and thanks- giving.

142. Besides consecrating the season to God, what other object has the Church in the Advent Ember Days?

She wishes to secure God's blessing on the ceremony of ordination, fixed for the Saturday of this week and (formerly at least) proclaimed to the people on Wednesday.

143. Is there anything special

A Catechism of the Liturgy

to the December ordination?

Yes, according to the directions of the early Popes, December was the only month during many centuries in which Holy Orders were conferred. Exceptions were made only for some extraordinary reason.

144. When the fourth Sunday and Christmas Eve coincide which takes precedence?

The vigil takes precedence.

145. Name some of the feasts which occur during Advent?

The feast of St. Andrew (November 30th) though it does not always occur in Advent will be found in the Missal at the opening of the Ecclesiastical year.

146. In order of time what feast comes next?

The feast of St. Francis Xavier

(December 3d). He is called the Apostle of the Indies; he converted hundreds in India, and when his mission was well established there, he longed to go to China, but he died on the Island of Sancian, within sight of his Promised Land.

147. What feasts are kept on December 8th and December 18th?

On December 8th the feast of the Immaculate Conception of Our Lady, and on the eighteenth the feast of the Expectation of Our Lady.

148. When was the dogma of the Immaculate Conception defined?

The dogma of the Immaculate Conception was defined an article of faith on December 8, 1854, by Pope Pius IX.

149. What do you mean by the "O Antiphons"?

The "O Antiphons" are special Antiphons sung at Vespers from the seventeenth to the twenty-fourth of December. They are so called because each one begins with the interjection O (e. g,, O wisdom proceeding from the mouth of the Almighty, etc.).

150. How is the vigil of Christmas Day spent?

In prayer and fasting but in the spirit of hope which sees its desires on the eve of fulfillment. If the vigil falls on Sunday, the office and Mass of the vigil are said in preference to those of the fourth Sunday.

CHRISTMAS

151. How does the Church celebrate the Midnight Birth?

By Midnight Mass, which the faithful as far as possible attend.

152. What special privilege is granted to priests for this feast?

Each priest is allowed to say three Masses in honor of the triple birth of Our Lord; 1st. His generation from Eternity from the Father. 2d. His birth as man. 3d. His birth in the souls of the faithful.

153. Has the privilege been extended to any other days?

Yes, the Holy Father extended the privilege to November 2nd since 1915, for the repose of the souls of those fallen in the War, and others according to his intentions.

154. Name some of the feasts which fall within the Octave of Christmas.

St. Stephen, St. John, The Holy

A Catechism of the Liturgy

Innocents, St. Thomas of Canterbury.

155. How does the Church show her sympathy with the mothers of the Holy Innocents?

She leaves aside the color of joy (white) and uses purple vestments which is the color of mourning. She also suppresses the Gloria (unless the feast falls on Sunday then the color of the vestments is red) and the Alleluias.[2]

156. How does the feast of St. Thomas of Canterbury differ from those we have been speaking about?

He does not belong to the first ages of the Church, neither is his name written in Scripture as those of the St. Stephen, St. John, and the

---

[2] In the 1962 rite, this has been changed. The color is red, and it now includes the Gloria.

Holy Innocents.

157. What are the next great feasts?

The feast of the Circumcision and the feast of the Epiphany, which are kept on January 1st and January 6th respectively.

158. What is the meaning of the word Epiphany?

The word Epiphany means "manifestation" and was chosen to signify God's showing Himself to man.

159. By what other name is the feast sometimes called?

It is sometimes called the feast of the Holy Lights, because it was one of the days chosen in the early Church for baptism, which is the sacrament of illumination, in memory of the baptism of Our Lord in the

Jordan which tradition fixed for January 6th.

160. Has it still another name?
Yes, it is familiarly called King's Day in honor of the Magi whose arrival in Bethlehem the Church commemorates on this day.

161. What is meant by the triple manifestation?
The three manifestations of Our Lord mentioned in the offices on this one feast, are: 1st. His manifestation to the Magi guided by a star which had led them to His abode in Bethlehem; 2d. The manifestation of His divinity declared by the voice of the Father at the Baptism in the Jordan; 3d. The manifestation of His Power in changing water into wine at the marriage feast of Cana.

162. How did Christian

Sovereigns once honor the faith of the Eastern kings?

By offering gifts of gold, incense and myrrh on the feast of the Epiphany.

163. Name some of the Sovereigns whom history records as faithful to the practice.

Theodosius and Charlemagne; Stephen of Hungary; Edward the Confessor; Ferdinand of Castille; Louis of France.

164. Name some of the feasts which fall between the Octave of the Epiphany and Septuagesima.

St. Paul the Hermit, St. Agnes, the Conversion of St. Paul, St. John Chrysostom, and St, Francis of Sales.

165. When is the feast of St. Agnes kept?

On January 21st, and on this day

the Church honors her name by blessing two lambs. These lambs are then sent to a Monastery of nuns, by whom the lambs are tended.

166. What is made with their wool?

From their wool are made the Palliums sent by the Holy Father as a sign of their jurisdiction to all Patriarchs and Archbishops throughout the Catholic world.

LENT

167. When is Septuagesima Sunday celebrated?

Septuagesima Sunday is the ninth Sunday before Easter. The Liturgy from this day forward is of a penitential character. The altar is unadorned, the hymn "Gloria in Excelsis" is not sung, and purple or violet colored vestments are used. Besides this the Hebrew ejaculation of praise "Alleluia" is omitted no matter how solemn be the feast that is celebrated.

168. What other changes appear in the Liturgy?

After the Gradual of the Mass a Tract, i.e., a series of verses from the psalms, is substituted for the Alleluia.

169. What does the word Lent mean?

Lent is an Anglo-Saxon word meaning Spring. It is the name given to the solemn fast observed by Catholics in preparation for Easter.

170. Is the practice of the Lenten fast an ancient one?

The Lenten fast dates back to Apostolic times as is attested by St. Jerome, St. Leo the Great, St. Cyril of

Alexandria and others.

171. What custom prevailed up to the ninth century?

Up to the ninth century it was the custom not to break the fast until sunset. After that it was allowed to break the fast at the hour of none, that is 3 o'clock in the afternoon, and in the twelfth century this had become general. In the fourteenth century it became the general custom to break the fast at midday.

172. What other custom prevailed in the Middle Ages during the time of Lent?

From the ninth century onwards it was forbidden to carry arms or wage war during Lent.

173. Of what are we reminded by the forty days of Lent?

In the fast of forty days we are

A Catechism of the Liturgy

reminded of the forty days deluge—the forty years wandering in the desert, the forty days fast of Moses before he received the Tables of the Law, the forty days fast of Elias—and Our Lord's fast of forty days.

174. Mention some of the Rites which formerly prevailed in the Western Church during Lent.

All during Lent an immense veil or screen of violet was hung between the choir and the altar, so that the faithful could no longer see the sacred Mysteries which were celebrated at the altar.

175. What did this veil symbolize?

This veil symbolized the mourning and spirit of penance of sinners who are not worthy to behold the Majesty of God. It also signified the humiliations of Christ, which veiled His divinity. This custom is still observed in the Metropolitan Church of Paris.

176. Did the Lenten fast always last forty days?

No, the length of the Lenten fast varied, and up to the time of Pope Gregory the Great, A. D. 600, lasted only thirty-six days and this older practice is still observed at Milan according to the Ambrosian Liturgy, but after the example set us by Our Lord Himself, a Lent of forty days has become practically universal.

177. From what ceremony does Ash Wednesday take its name?

Ash Wednesday takes its name from the ceremony of the faithful receiving ashes on that day, which is a vestige of the primitive rite, when public sinners did penance each year in sack-cloth and ashes.

178. How are the ashes obtained for the ceremony of Ash Wednesday?

The Rubrics prescribe that the ashes used on this day, should be obtained by the burning of the palms blessed on Palm Sunday of the year before.

179. When do the Lenten Ember Days occur?

The Lenten Ember Days are on the Wednesday, Friday and Saturday after the first Sunday in Lent.

180. What is meant by Ember Days?

The Ember Days (called in Latin "Quatuor Tempora") are the Wednesdays, Fridays and Saturdays of four weeks taken in each of the four seasons of the year and set apart as days of strict fasting and abstinence.

181. When did they originate?

They originated in Rome at the time of the Emperor Constantine. They were first days of prayer and later were chosen as the regular days for giving Holy Orders.

182. What addition is there to the Mass on the Ember Wednesdays, and Saturdays?

Two or more Epistles or Lessons are added, together with additional prayers or Collects.

183. What is there to be noticed about the fourth Sunday in Lent?

On the fourth Sunday in Lent which is called Mid-Lent Sunday, the Liturgical austerity of Lent is somewhat relaxed. The altar is adorned with flowers, the organ is played, and the priest may wear rose-colored vestments instead of violet ones.

184. What custom is observed at Rome on this Sunday?

On the fourth Sunday of Lent the Pope blesses a rose made *of* gold, known as the Golden Rose, and carries it himself in procession. The rose is afterwards bestowed as a mark of special favor on some remarkable personage.

185. What is Passion Sunday?

Passion Sunday is the fifth Sunday in Lent. From this date the Preface of the Holy Cross is said daily at Mass, and as in Masses for the dead the Psalm, "Judica me" and the "Gloria Patri" are omitted.

186. What striking practice is

A Catechism of the Liturgy

customary in the churches from Passion Sunday to the end of Lent?

The crosses, statues and pictures in the churches are all veiled from Passion Sunday till Holy Saturday.

187. Why are they covered?

All crosses and images are covered during Passiontide to inspire the faithful with greater compunction, in being deprived of the consolation of seeing these objects of devotion.

188. What Feasts of Saints usually occur during Lent?

St. Matthias, Apostle, February 24th or 25th; St. Thomas Aquinas, Doctor of the Church, March 7th; St. Gregory the Great, Pope and Doctor, March 12th; St. Patrick, Apostle of Ireland, March 17th; St. Joseph, March 19th; St. Benedict, March 21st;

St. Leo the Great, Pope and Doctor, April 11th.

189. When the Feast of St. Joseph and the Annunciation of Our Lady fall in Passiontide when are they kept?

The feast of St. Joseph is transferred to Wednesday in Low Week and the Annunciation to Monday in Low Week.

HOLY WEEK

190. Why is Holy Week so called?

It is so called on account of the grandeur and holiness of the great mysteries which it commemorates.

191. Since when has Holy Week been set apart for special veneration by the faithful?

In the third century it was already in great veneration, and in the fourth century St. John Chrysostom speaks of it in one of his homilies as "the Great Week."

192. How does the Church prepare us by her Liturgy for the celebration of the Passion in Holy Week?

The "Gloria Patri" is no longer said. The Lamentations of Jeremias are sung at the evening office. The vestments of violet are changed for black on Good Friday. The crosses are veiled and the statues and pictures also.

193. Why is Palm Sunday so called and what mysteries are commemorated on that day?

It is so called because palms are solemnly blessed on that day and distributed to the faithful in memory of Our Lord's entry into Jerusalem on the colt of an ass.

194. What meaning do the Fathers of the Church give to the use of these animals?

The ass represents the Jews who had been long under the yoke of the Law, and the colt "upon which no man yet hath sat" represents the Gentiles.

195. What Gospel is read on Palm Sunday and what is the meaning of the procession on that day?

The Gospel of St. Matthew is read at Mass on Palm Sunday because St. Matthew was the first Evangelist to write the Passion, and the procession in memory of the deliverance of the Jews from their slavery in Egypt and of their entrance into the Promised Land. It signifies also Christ's triumphal entry into Jerusalem.

196. Why is the office of Tenebrae so called?

Tenebrae means darkness, and it is so called from the ceremony of extinguishing the candles during it, till at last it is finished in total darkness recalling that of Calvary.

197. What is the meaning of the candles lighted during Tenebrae?

They mean the light of faith; the Mystery of the Blessed Trinity being symbolized by the triangular candlestick.

198. When are these candles extinguished?

At the end of each of the fourteen Psalms a candle of the triangular candlestick is extinguished, and a candle on the altar at the end of every second verse of the Benedictus, showing how the Jews were deprived of the light of faith when they put Our Lord to death. The fifteenth candle representing the Light of the world is hidden for a time behind the altar and brought out at the end of Tenebrae still burning.

199. On which days of Holy Week are the other three Gospels of the Passion read?

St. Mark's Gospel is read on Tuesday, St. Luke's on Wednesday, and St. John's on Good Friday.

200. In olden times how many Masses were celebrated on Maundy Thursday?

Three solemn Masses were celebrated. Before the first there took place the ceremony of the "reconciliation of the penitents." The second Mass was accompanied with the blessing of the Holy Oils (and Chrism). The third Mass which is the only one said in our days, is in memory of the Last Supper and the Institution of the Blessed Sacrament. It is one of the most solemn of the whole year.

201. Why are there fewer Masses on Maundy Thursday?

The Church wishing to bring before us the grandeur and unity of the Last Supper given by Our Lord to His Apostles and in their persons to us all, forbids the celebration of private Masses on this day unless in a case of great necessity. Only one Mass is offered in each church at which all the priests assist and communicate, wearing the stole symbol of the priestly office.

202. In what does this Mass differ from the others in Holy

Week?

Though the office of this day is of the Passion, the Mass is of the Holy Eucharist and is therefore filled with joy and thanksgiving. The vestments are white like those worn on Christmas Day and Easter Sunday the "Gloria in Excelsis" is sung during which the bells joyfully peal.

203. Why are the bells and the organ silent after the Gloria?

The silence is to honor Our Lord's silence during His Passion and also to express the mourning of the Church.

204. Why is the kiss of peace not given as is usual at a High Mass?

This is to remind us of Judas, who chose this sign of friend-ship, a kiss, with which to betray Our Lord, and the Church wishes to remind us of this traitorous act.

205. What do the Rubrics prescribe on this day at the consecration?

That two Hosts should be consecrated, one for the sacrifice of the Mass, the other for Good Friday.

206. What is done with the second Host?

After Mass It is borne in solemn procession to a side-altar or Repository decorated with lights and flowers, where It remains for the adoration of the faithful until Good Friday morning.

207. What is the meaning of stripping the altars after Vespers?

This ceremony refers to the stripping of Our Savior's garments and the bareness of the altars signifies that in His Passion He lost all His beauty and comeliness. The priest and choir say or chant the twenty-first Psalm, "Deus, Deus meus during the ceremony.

208. How is the Blessed Sacrament carried to the altar of repose?

The Blessed Sacrament is not carried in a monstrance as on the feast of Corpus Christi, but in a chalice veiled in white silk. The faithful follow, carrying candles and singing the "Pange Lingua."

209. What is the ceremony of the "Mandatum"?

The washing of the feet called in the Rubrics "Mandatum," or "The Commandment," owes its institution to the words and example of Our Savior when He washed the Apostles' feet before the Institution of the Blessed Sacrament. It reminds us to imitate Our Lord's humility in offices of charity, as well as to cleanse our souls from the stains of sin.

210. Is there any other reason why this ceremony is called the "Mandatum"?

Yes, it is so called because the first word of the Antiphon sung during the washing of the feet begins with the word "Mandatum," taken from the Gospel of the day.

211. Is this custom of ancient origin?

Yes, St. Paul speaks of it as one of the holy widows' offices to the Saints. It was customary in the times of the martyrs. In the Lives of the Saints frequent allusions are made to it, and today the Holy Father gives the example to the whole Church, which is followed by Bishops and Catholic sovereigns as in ancient times.

212. Who are generally chosen to take part in this ceremony?

Twelve poor people are chosen, but the Holy Father washes the feet of thirteen priests of thirteen different nations. In Cathedral Churches thirteen is the number chosen.

213. What is the reason for this number?

It is supposed to arise from an incident in the life of St. Gregory the Great; one day as he was washing the feet of twelve beggars, a thirteenth was found among them. He had entered unperceived and was an angel sent by God to show how pleasing to Him was St. Gregory's charity.

214. What pious custom is there of honoring the Blessed Sacrament on Maundy Thursday?

It is customary to pay seven visits to the altar of repose on this day, either to seven different churches or to one, and in religious houses there is night-adoration.

215. What are the principal ceremonies on Good Friday?

The Divine service is divided into four parts: 1. There is reading of prophecies; 2. then follow the beautiful prayers in supplication for all men imploring that the fruit of the Passion may be applied to all; 3. after these prayers there is Adoration of the Cross; 4. the Mass of the Presanctified.

216. Why is the Mass so called?

The Mass of the Presanctified is so called because the priest does not consecrate on Good Friday, but consumes the second Host, which he consecrated during the Mass on Maundy Thursday.

217. Which are the principal ceremonies on Holy Saturday?

On this day the altars deprived of their ornaments on Maundy Thursday are again clothed. The office begins with the lighting of a triple candle to signify the light of Christ and the mystery of the Blessed Trinity.

218. What special blessings precede the office of Holy Saturday?

Outside the Church door the celebrant and deacons go to a place prepared for the blessing of the new fire and incense. The fire represents Christ risen from the tomb outside the Gates of Jerusalem, hence the reason that fire is blessed outside the Church.

219. When is the Paschal Candle blessed and what does it

signify?

The Paschal Candle is blessed by the deacon before the office and is a figure of the Body of Jesus Christ; not lighted at first, it represents Him dead and the five blessed grains of incense fixed in it denote the aromatic spices that embalmed His five Sacred Wounds.

220. What does the lighting of the Paschal Candle signify?

It is a representation of Our Lord's Resurrection, and the lighting of the lamps and other candles afterwards teaches us that the Resurrection of the Head will be followed by that of the members.

221. What other special blessing takes place on Holy Saturday?

The baptismal font is also blessed with very beautiful and sacred ceremonies.

222. Does Mass begin immediately after the blessing of the new fire?
No, the celebrant now changes his white vestments for a pur- ple chasuble and reads twelve Prophecies in a low voice at the Epistle comer of the altar while one or more deacons in turn read them aloud in the church.

223. Why are the Prophecies read before Mass?
The Prophecies are read before Mass because in olden times the neophytes received baptism, and the Prophecies, each followed by a prayer, were read during the long baptismal rites.

224. What follows the reading of the Prophecies?

The priests and deacons sing the Litany of the Saints prostrate on the altar steps, to implore heavenly blessing on the neophytes in the different parts of the world.

225. What takes place immediately after the Litany?

While the deacons are singing the last "Kyrie Eleison," the celebrant goes up to the altar clad in white vestments. He incenses the altar and intones the "Gloria," then the bells ring, the organ peals and the church is flooded with light.

EASTER TO ADVENT

226. What is the origin of the word Easter?

The word Easter in the English language is said by St. Bede to be of pagan origin, but by a coincidence of dates has been, by the Teutonic and other peoples whose language they have influenced, preserved to denote the feast of the Resurrection. In other languages a word is employed derived from the word *Pasch*, or Passover, e.g. Latin: *Pascha*, which predates the English usage by centuries.

227. When is the feast kept?

Easter is kept on the first Sunday following the full moon after March 21st. The earliest possible Easter day is March 22d, the latest, April 25th.

228. What is the distinctive feature of the Easter rite?

The constant repeating of the word "Alleluia," the Hebrew shout of joy, which means "Praise the Lord."

229. Why is the following Sunday called Low Sunday?

Low Sunday is so called by contrast with Easter or High Sunday; it has this name, however, only in English. In the Liturgy it is called "Dominica in Albis," Sunday in white garments, seeing that those baptized on Holy Saturday laid aside the evening before this day their white robes worn since then.

230. What are the Rogation Days?

Monday, Tuesday and Wednesday before Ascension Day are called Rogation Days from the Latin word signifying Asking or Petitioning. The Roman Church, in the eighth century, set them apart as days of special prayer for the fruits of the earth. On each day the Litany of the Saints is sung or said.

231. Are they fast days?

There are no fasts between Easter

and Whitsun Eve in memory of the word of Our Lord: "Can the children of the Bridegroom fast whilst the Bridegroom is with them?"

232. What special ceremony is there on Ascension Day?

On Ascension Day the Paschal Candle is extinguished. It has burned during Mass for forty days since Easter, symbolizing the life upon earth of the risen Christ.

233. What likeness is there between Whitsun Eve and Holy Saturday?

Like Holy Saturday, Whitsun Eve was set apart by the primitive Church for the administration of solemn baptism. Six prophecies are read, the font is blessed, the Litany of the Saints sung, and bells are rung at the "Gloria."

234. Whence the name of Whitsunday?

It is so called in English in allusion to the white robes of the newly baptized, the Ecclesiastical name is Pentecost.

235. What is the meaning of the word Pentecost?

The word Pentecost means fiftieth. It is the Jewish Feast of Weeks, celebrated on the fiftieth day after the Pasch and made sacred to Christians by the coming down of the Holy Ghost on the Apostles.

236. Why are the vestments red on Whitsunday?

The vestments on Whitsunday are red in memory of the Holy Ghost having come down in the form of tongues of fire.

237. What is the Octave day of

Whitsunday called?

The Octave day of Whitsunday is called Trinity Sunday, as it is celebrated in honor of the Holy and Undivided Trinity.

238. Why is a feast kept in honor of the Blessed Sacrament on the following Thursday as well as on Maundy Thursday?

Maundy Thursday is partly taken up with commemoration of the Passion and therefore the Church cannot rejoice as fully as she would wish to do in the thought of the institution of the Holy Eucharist. We owe the feast to a vision of St. Juliana of Liège.

239. Is there any great feast kept at this time?

The Friday after the Octave of Corpus Christi is consecrated to the Sacred Heart in response to an appeal for reparation made by Our Lord to St. Margaret Mary.

240. How many Sundays after Pentecost are there?

The least number is twenty-four. If Easter has been an early one and the Sundays after Epiphany omitted, these are inserted after the twenty-third Sunday.

241. What feasts of Our Lady are kept between March 22d and December 1st?

The greatest feast is that of the Annunciation, called in England, Lady Day, March 25th. It is kept in honor of the announcement made by the Archangel Gabriel to Our Lady of the Incarnation of the Son of God.

242. What lesser feast do we keep in her honor?

Our Lady Help of Christians, May

24th, instituted in thanksgiving by Pope Pius VII for the end of the exile of the Sovereign Pontiffs; the Visitation, July 2d; Mount Carmel, July 16th; her Nativity, September 8th.

243. Are any of Our Lady's feasts Holy days of obligation?

Yes, the feast of the Assumption of her body into Heaven, which we keep August 15th, is a holyday of obligation, and the Immaculate Conception, December 8th.

244. Name some other feasts in honor of Mary at this time of the year?

The Immaculate Heart on the Saturday following the Octave of the Assumption and the Holy Name of Mary, September 12th, instituted in thanksgiving for the defeat of the Turks at Vienna by Sobieski and the deliverance of Europe from the infidels.

245. Why is the Litany of the Saints sung on the feast of St. Mark, April 25th?

This day sacred to the gods of Pagan Rome was by some of the early Popes set apart as a day of special prayer for the averting of God's anger, and the imploring of His blessing on the labors of the year. St. Gregory the Great obtained on this day the miraculous cessation of a terrible plague.

246. Why are some feasts, such as those of the Apostles said to have vigils?

A vigil means a watch. The early Christians spent the eve of the feast in prayer and watching. All vigils were formerly fast days.

247. Why is the Nativity of St. John the Baptist kept on June 24th, whilst no other Saint's birthday is kept?

Because, unlike all other saints who were born in original sin, the birth of St. John was holy owing to the visit of our Blessed Lady.

248. Is there any reason for the single feast of SS. Peter and Paul?

SS. Peter and Paul were both martyred on the same day at Rome, St. Peter crucified, St. Paul beheaded. Now, one is never mentioned without the other.

249. What is Petertide?

The time between the Feast of St. Peter, June 29th, and the Feast of his Chains, August 1st, is called Petertide.

250. Why is this latter day

A Catechism of the Liturgy

called Lammas?

At the Altar of St. Peter at Vincula where his chains are kept, it was formerly the custom on this day to offer the first bread baked from the wheat harvest of the year. This gave to the feast its popular name of "Loaf-Mass" or Lammas.

251. Why is the Creed said at Mass on the feast of St. Mary Magdalene, alone of all women saints?

Because she is styled by the Church "the Apostle of the Apostles," being sent by Our Lord to them to announce His Resurrection.

252. When is the feast of the Seven Dolors of Mary?

The Seven Dolors of Mary are commemorated on September 15th. This is one of the few Masses that has a Sequence, viz., the Stabat

Mater.

253. What feast is kept on September 14th?

The feast of the Exaltation of the Holy Cross to commemorate the victory of the Emperor Heraclius over the Persians when he recovered the True Cross from their possession, and carried it in triumph to Jerusalem.

254. What is the special devotion of October?

The Rosary recited in common to obtain perfect liberty for the Holy Father.

255. Why do we keep one feast in honor of all the Saints on November 1st?

To honor all those in Heaven, canonized or uncanonized. It is a day of rejoicing in the Communion of

Saints. Because of this same communion the following day we commemorate all the faithful departed who are still suffering in Purgatory and we try to assist them by our prayers.

FINIS